Extreme Sports

SURFING

Matt Scheff

DiscoverRoo
An Imprint of Pop!
popbooksonline.com

abdobooks.com

Published by Pop!, a division of ABDO, PO Box 398166, Minneapolis, Minnesota 55439.

Printed in the United States of America, North Mankato, Minnesota.

052020
092020

THIS BOOK CONTAINS RECYCLED MATERIALS

Cover Photo: Meibion/Alamy

Interior Photos: Meibion/Alamy, 1; iStockphoto, 5, 6, 11, 15, 16, 17, 20, 21, 22, 27, 28, 30; Shutterstock Images, 7, 8–9, 19, 25, 29, 31; Alpha Historica/Alamy, 12, 13; Martin James Brannan/Fairfax Media Archives/Getty Images, 14; Red Line Editorial, 23

Editor: Brienna Rossiter
Series Designer: Jake Slavik

Library of Congress Control Number: 2019954958

Publisher's Cataloging-in-Publication Data

Names: Scheff, Matt, author.

Title: Surfing / by Matt Scheff

Description: Minneapolis, Minnesota : POP!, 2021 | Series: Extreme sports | Includes online resources and index.

Identifiers: ISBN 9781532167881 (lib. bdg.) | ISBN 9781532168987 (ebook)

Subjects: LCSH: Surfing--Juvenile literature. | Surfboarders--Juvenile literature. | Aquatic sports--Juvenile literature. | Extreme sports--Juvenile literature. | Sports--Juvenile literature.

Classification: DDC 796.046--dc23

WELCOME TO DiscoverRoo!

Pop open this book and you'll find QR codes loaded with information, so you can learn even more!

Scan this code* and others like it while you read, or visit the website below to make this book pop!

popbooksonline.com/surfing

*Scanning QR codes requires a web-enabled smart device with a QR code reader app and a camera.

TABLE OF CONTENTS

CHAPTER 1

CATCHING WAVES

A surfer paddles in the warm water near a beach in Hawaii. Waves crash against the sand behind her. The surfer floats on her board. She watches for the perfect wave to ride back to shore.

WATCH A VIDEO HERE!

Surfers catch waves at the surf line. This is the area where waves begin to break as they near the shore.

A surfer does a pop-up to get to her feet. This move is similar to a fast push-up.

Finally, she spots what she's looking for. A long, tall wave is heading toward her. As it gets closer, the surfer paddles to pick up speed. When the wave catches her, she stands up quickly. The wave's power sweeps her along.

Surfers shift back and forth along their boards as they ride waves.

Hang ten **is a popular surfing term. It means to surf with all ten toes at the front of the surfboard.**

Soon, the wave begins to **break**. The surfer rides through the tunnel of water as long as she can. Eventually, she

A barrel is the tunnel of water that forms when a wave breaks. Surfing inside it is called tube riding.

falls off her board. But she swims to the surface and climbs back on. Then she paddles out to catch another wave.

CHAPTER 2

HISTORY OF SURFING

Surfing has its roots in ancient Polynesia. Polynesia is a group of islands located in the Pacific Ocean. People there began surfing thousands of years ago. They

LEARN MORE HERE!

This picture from 1882 shows people surfing in Polynesia.

used wooden boards. Surfing became a big part of many Polynesian **cultures**. This was especially true in Hawaii. Nearly everyone who lived there surfed. Its rulers even hosted contests.

Duke Kahanamoku helped make surfing popular in the early 1900s. He was also an Olympic swimmer.

In the late 1800s, Hawaiians brought surfing to California. The sport spread quickly. Surfers flocked to beaches in California and Australia. Movies and songs about surfing helped make it even more popular.

Newport Harbor in California became a popular surfing spot in the 1930s.

Margo Oberg was the first female professional surfer.

By the mid-1900s, surfing had become a competitive sport. The first West Coast Surfing Championships took place in 1959. And the United States

Surfing Association (USSA) formed in 1961.

Fans loved watching surfers compete.

DID YOU KNOW?

Surfing is not just for people. There have been dog surfing competitions since the 1920s.

Several beaches in California hold dog surfing competitions each year.

Over the years, surfboard designs changed. They became smaller, lighter, and easier to **maneuver**. Surfers could do a wide range of twists and turns.

SURFBOARD SHAPES

Long ago, all surfers used longboards. These surfboards were more than 7 feet (2.1 m) long. In the 1960s, shortboards became popular. These boards are less than 7 feet (2.1 m) long. Surfboard materials have changed too. Instead of wood, most modern boards use fiberglass. This material is lighter and stronger.

Most modern surfboards have three fins near the back.

CHAPTER 3

THE SPORT TODAY

Today, people ride waves at beaches all around the world. Modern surfboards have fins on the bottom. The fins help keep the boards steady. They also help surfers control their speed and direction.

COMPLETE AN ACTIVITY HERE!

A leash should be at least as long as the surfboard.

A leash attaches the board to the surfer's ankle. That way, the board can't float away and leave the surfer stranded.

Hawaii hosts several major surfing events. Other top competitions take place in Australia.

Many of the best surfers compete. At competitions, surfers have a set amount of time, often 20 to 30 minutes, to catch waves. Judges score each surfer's two best rides. Surfers get points based on the quality of the wave and how well they surf it. They look for big waves with long **barrels**.

In 2018, Rodrigo Koxa set a world record by surfing an 80-foot (24-m) wave. That's taller than a 7-story building!

Surfers do tricks as they ride each wave. They **carve** and **trim**. Or they fly above the water with **aerials**. Some surfers can spin their boards all the way around. This trick is called a 360.

Many tricks require surfers to do quick turns.

SURFING TERMS

drop:
moving down the wave

aerial:
a move where the surfer flies up off the wave

frontside:
surfing facing the wave

cutback:
turning from the top of the wave back down toward the wave's breaking part

backside:
surfing facing away from the wave

bottom turn:
a curve done at the wave's base so the surfer can move along the wave

SUPERSTAR

STEPHANIE GILMORE

- Stephanie Gilmore grew up in Australia. She started surfing when she was 11.
- In 2007, Gilmore won a world title during her first year competing as a pro. No surfer had done this before. But the 19-year-old was just getting started. She won three more world titles in a row. And by 2018, she had a total of seven.
- Gilmore won the Laureus World Sports Award in 2010. This is the biggest award for action sports.

In 2012, Stephanie Gilmore earned her fifth world title at the Roxy Pro Biarritz in France.

- She's working to change the sport so that female surfers, who often earn less than male surfers, can receive equal pay and prize money.
- In addition to surfing, Gilmore loves music. She plays guitar and even performs sometimes.

CHAPTER 4

SURFING SAFELY

Deep water and big waves make safety a big concern for surfers. Beaches use flags and signs to post warnings. Some tell when waves are too strong. Others tell if there are sharks.

LEARN MORE HERE!

Colored flags tell the strength of the wind and currents each day.

Lifeguards watch over surfers at Bondi Beach in Australia.

Surfers should always obey these warnings. They should stay out of dangerous water. And they should never surf alone. If a surfer has an accident, it's important to have others there to help.

Surfers gather at Praia do Norte in Portugal to ride some of the biggest waves in the world.

DID YOU KNOW?

In big wave surfing, people ride waves that are more than 20 feet (6.1 m) tall. These surfers need extra experience and training.

MAKING CONNECTIONS

TEXT-TO-SELF

Would you want to surf at a beach in Hawaii? Why or why not?

TEXT-TO-TEXT

Have you read about other sports or activities that involve water? In what parts of the world are those activities common?

TEXT-TO-WORLD

How might surfing have been different in ancient times? How might it be different in the future?

GLOSSARY

aerial – a trick where a surfer flies off the top of a wave and into the air.

barrel – the hollow, tube-shaped tunnel of water created when a wave breaks.

break – when a wave curls over, sending a spray of water crashing down.

carve – to turn sharply by leaning back so only the edge of the surfboard touches the water.

culture – the ideas, lifestyle, and traditions of a group of people.

maneuver – to move with great skill or control.

trim – to move higher or lower along a wave.

INDEX

ONLINE RESOURCES

popbooksonline.com

Scan this code* and others like it while you read, or visit the website below to make this book pop!

popbooksonline.com/surfing

*Scanning QR codes requires a web-enabled smart device with a QR code reader app and a camera.